No More Insecurities Guide

How to stop Negative thinking in a few steps.
Avoid problems, eliminate negative people
and start a new happy life. Overcome Jealousy
and develop healthy communication

Philip Steiner

TABLE OF CONTENTS

INTRODUCTION

Thank you for purchasing this book, I am sure you will find all the answers you are looking for to break down jealousy, negative thoughts etc.

Unfortunately, jealousy is almost always due to poor communication with your partner, so the advice I can give you is to listen to your partner more, to give him more attention and above all to always love yourself first to ensure that others love you.

Now I leave you to your reading, here you will find all the useful tips to overcome all your difficulties to live a peaceful life away from anxiety, jealousy and negative thoughts.

Enjoy!

CHAPTER 1 - Transform Your New Communication Skills in Healthy Habits

Learning how to communicate in a supportive and healthy way with your partner is the foundation for a long-lasting and enjoyable relationship. However, to truly gain the most out of your relationship, you must learn beyond the conversation. It is great to talk about things, but there is more to a relationship than just talking. For a relationship to end a lifetime, we need to show our love to our partners and be conscious of our actions.

Pierre Reverdy once said, "There is no love. There are only proofs of love." Whatever love we feel towards someone is ultimately meaningless unless we do things to prove our love.

This is especially important when a relationship has evolved past the honeymoon phase. The grind of everyday life, work, children, chores, and family commitments all impact our relationship. You might not forget to say "I love you" to your partner when they go to work or when you hang up the phone, but after a while, this phrase might feel meaningless and more of a habit than any actual declaration of love. To keep love alive, both people in the relationship need to be aware of body language and actions, both intentionally and unintentionally.

Intentional Actions

We have all heard the phrase, "Actions speak louder than words." This is true concerning most things in life, but especially true in relationships. We can say we love, respect, and support our partner until we are blue in the face, but it all comes down to our actions. We all have been there for a friend who is in an unhealthy relationship and witnessed how words can be meaningless. Your friend might say that her boyfriend cheated on her or stood her up on a date. He might then apologize and tell her that he loves her. But this is meaningless. His actions have not proved his love for her. Therefore, the words he is saying do not matter. Similarly, someone might feel unsupported by their partner even if they claim to be supportive. Telling your partner, "I support you in your goal to be an artist," is meaningless if you do not look at their art and attend galleries with them.

To make a relationship work, we need to back up our love with intentional actions.

Using Love Languages

Think back to the five love languages. Four out of five love languages rely on actions rather than words, showing that these are very important in a relationship. Using these can improve a relationship and show your partner that you love them.

Jane and Becky did an online test for their love languages. Both had words of affirmation as their most important one, and therefore they took it upon themselves to be vocal about their love and support for one another. It has helped the relationship; however, Becky feels that there is still something lacking and wants Jane to show her more love in different ways.

She retakes the love language test, and words of affirmation came out on top again, but she looks at her second love language. She sees it is physical touch. She tells Jane this and suggests that actions are also necessary for their relationship. They build on this, using physical touch to show each other their love.

Their situation shows that even if your love language is words of affirmation, it is essential to pay attention to others. Words are essential for most couples, but a balance between actions and words can maintain an honest and loving relationship. Showing your love might make your partner feel ten times more loved than merely telling them.

Paying Attention

How often do you feel your partner is not listening to you? This is a common complaint in couples that have been together for a while. However, it does not mean that your partner is not listening. When you are used to each other and know each other well, you become more in tune with their thoughts and feelings. This might mean that you find it easy to only half-listen to what they are saying, as you know, their train of thought and how they react to certain situations. But, this can become an issue in a relationship. There is no malice or harmful intentions in this, but it can create feelings of resentment and sadness. Your partner might not feel you love them as much as you once did. They might worry that they bore you, and that is not fair to them. However, we can use our actions to show that we are paying attention to our partners. When you sit on the sofa and talk with your partner, turn towards them to show that you are paying attention. Put a hand on their leg, maintain eye contact. Nods and words of encouragement or agreement can help your partner know that you listen to them. In paying attention to your partner, you show your love to them using both conversational and physical tools. Paying attention is not just about showing you are listening to them. You can also use other actions to give your partner attention and show that you love them. Giving your partner attention in a physical yet non-sexual way is a great and easy way to pay attention to them. Hand holding is the perfect and most straightforward way of providing a physical action that shows love and support. Closeness and cuddles on the sofa in front of the TV can be both relaxing and supportive.

When out shopping, an arm around your partner when browsing the aisles is another small but effective way of showing love.

Remember Jane and Becky, whose love language was both words of affirmation. When they discovered and mentioned their love languages, Becky had been laid-off and was looking for a job. This had affected her self-esteem and self-worth, and Jane, knowing that her love language was words of affirmation, told Becky multiple times a day that she was generous, smart, and hardworking. She told her that she would soon find a new job.

Unintentional Actions

We have looked at intentional actions to support our partners, but we also need to be aware of unintentional actions that can negatively affect our relationships. We may be telling our partners we love them but have actions that suggest otherwise. These actions are not intentional, but still push your partner away. It is vital to be aware of body language and physical space in a relationship. By knowing these things, you can avoid unnecessary conflict.

Body Language

Body language is the language all humans speak. Energy and attitude come from how we hold ourselves, and negative body language can make or break a relationship. Most communication does come from our body language as we use our bodies to convey meaning and emotion.

Imagine sitting on the sofa with your partner. You have hunched away from them, arms folded, looking the opposite way. You say, "I love you." Do you expect your partner to feel loved? Now picture you sitting on the sofa with them, but in this instance, you are turned towards your partner, an arm around their shoulders, gazing into their eyes. You say, "I love you."

In both instances, you have said the same thing, but the meaning is entirely different. This is solely because of your body language. For your relationship to be long-lasting and robust, you need to be aware of your body language and tell your partner.

Most body language we use is unintentional. We do not realize that our bodies tell our partners what we are feeling, even if our mouths say something different. We might also mean what we are telling our partners, but our bodies are not in tune with our thoughts. A lot of the time, this is in reaction to past relationships. We learn body language through other people and take this on without meaning to. A woman who has been frightened of a past partner is more likely to use closed-off body language to their current partner. She probably does not mean to do this, but it harms her current relationship.

Body language can start as a reaction to something small, but can grow to become a severe relationship. The energy and vibes that come from our bodies can linger and be repeated. Therefore, it is necessary to be aware of our unintentional body language and be active in changing it.

A waitress in a busy restaurant passes the time by polishing glasses and watching couples eating their meals. She enjoys this part of the job, watching romance blossom. She can quickly tell who is on their first date, their second date, or fiftieth. The restaurant is loud, with music playing, people chattering and clanging and shouting coming from the kitchen. This means that she can't hear what is being said at each restaurant table, but she can watch them. She has soon learned that watching people's body language tells her more about them than eavesdropping into conversations.

There are two tables by the window, and each table has a couple sitting down and enjoying their meal. She watches them. The couple on the left is leaning over the table to each other. Their hands are on the table and occasionally brush against one another. They are gazing into each other's eyes, and the waitress even notices the woman resting her feet against the man's leg underneath the table. They seem oblivious to the rest of the restaurant, only looking away from each other to order or thank the waitress for their food.

The couple on the right has an entirely different energy. The man is sitting back from the table, his arms folded, staring down at his plate. The woman gazes around the restaurant, picking at her food, arms, and legs tucked in towards her body.

Both couples have entirely different body languages. The waitress can clearly understand their situations, even though the only words she has heard them say were when they ordered their food. Now, following time you are at a restaurant with your significant other, try and think about which couple you are, the one on the left or the one on the right? The waitress assumed the couple on the left had only just started dating, but she was wrong for the first time! This couple had been dating twice as long as the couple on the right, and they were out to celebrate their twentieth wedding anniversary. They, however, knew the importance of body language to show each other their love. It is not only the honeymooners that can be all gooey and romantic!

CHAPTER 2 - Keep Love Alive for Long Term

Love is the glue that keeps marriages together. When you use up all your love, your union either crumbles, or you also grow to be a miserable individual; equally horrible options. Therefore, it's crucial to know about methods of keeping your love alive for the very long run.

Do Not Quit Dating

After you met each other, you were able to strike the restaurants to perform cocktails and dinner. However, when you have married, the dates ceased, and residence life happened. You know what? You should not have stopped communicating. It's true, you're married, but you can keep heading out on a couple of dates. You do not necessarily need to go to fancy restaurants. You may revive your chemical and generate a segment where you could have dates that survive even a whole day. If you like someone, you can always talk about a relationship together. However, that is insufficient. To be able to be profoundly connected, you'll need to use a bit of creativity. Thus, make sure that you're employing your creativity in your union to maintain the love alive.

Do Not Quit Going On Honeymoons

We're all about breaking the rules. Who states newlyweds have a monopoly of honeymoons? Even couples who've been together for ages ought to opt for honeymoons whenever they would like to. Each year make sure that you and you are significantly additional traveling away for your honeymoon. Leave the children behind. Such experiences can allow you to know one yet be the very best couple. Honeymoons are costly if you're traveling abroad and staying in five-star resorts. However, you don't have to cross continents to get the honeymoon. If you lack the financial burden of travel abroad, just search for a tranquil place, and proceed by train or automobile.

Unplug from Societal Networking

Social media is accountable for the passing of several unions. Because of sites such as Facebook and Twitter, individuals are now competing with a worldwide audience, as every one of them struggles to clearly show their awesomeness, their ideal candy heart, their great union, etc. So, when folks log on Facebook and watch these images, it tugs in their self-esteem. Social networking is teeming with busybodies that have nothing to do with their own lives, so they lead to generating play. To steer clear of racing against other people, you may want to uninstall these social networking programs and be accurate with your spouse.

Take A Bath Together

Simple things, such as taking a bath together, may have a profound impact on a few. The beauty of this is it is free. And you're able to embark on this action daily. As you are a fan, do not be terrified of extending your creativity. Take turns washing each other. When you bathe her back, then she pays by scrubbing your thighs and then washing your spine. Make it as entertaining as it could be. Daily after work, you will arrange to get a sea salt bath, then proceed to a candle-lit bedroom to get magical nighttime. Making such authentic experiences brings a few nearer to one another.

Feed One Another

When you head out on dates from fancy restaurants, you wish to be the few standing outside, but for a good reason: feeding on your partner just like a tiny baby. Sit across from each other at relatively tiny tables. And possess the "baby" of their afternoon fold their hands around their chest as the "momma" feeds her together with her folk, or even in extreme instances, slips across the desk and administers food out of their mouth as if swallowing a toothless infant.

Get Lost in Your Partner's Eyes

Produce a habit of dig deep into your partner's eyes, so deep that you can see your spirit. However, before you do this, you wish to ensure that the environment is simply perfect. Create a pleasant and trendy ambiance. Have your spouse recline in a chair? And after that, it is possible to slim down and stare into their eyes. Ensure there is some mild background audio to improve the mood.

Dance

Who says you have to have functional dancing abilities before you dancing? After dinner, then go across the table, select your spouse's hand and then draw them into the dancing floor. Dance your sorrows away. You might even get in the practice of randomly catching your partner and engaging them at a dancing. Simple things such as dance bring a few closer to one another.

Text Each Other

When you've got one another, you don't have any reason to seek expensive massage services again. You merely need to straddle your spouse's spine and work for your hands throughout their entire body, using ample amounts of massage oil. They'll uuuh and ahhh because you grace your palms out of one part to another. Massages also aid a few to comprehend what each individual's body resembles. Not to mention, you will encounter a part that appears nonhuman. But researching your spouse's body for a very long time offers you a glimpse into their unique traits, for instance, their bizarre erogenous zones.

Read Love Poems

Many famous men and women that were into adore were also large on poetry. William Shakespeare, Winston Churchill, William Faulkner... All these were accomplished guys that loved girls and loved reading poems. Of training course, not every single individual enjoys poetry.

However, you would not know if you love or despise it unless you attempted. Thus, get in the habit of reading every other gender. It's an excellent way of killing time and getting bogged into the ideal mood for revived sex.

Write To Each Other Love Letters

A love letter is just something to be appreciated. They communicate feelings in their rawest form. Thus, why not get in the practice of composing another love letter and then conceal them in lively places? Does this make it feel like living in precisely the same home and writing every other love letters? Yes, it will! If you discover ink and paper usage somewhat bothersome, then you always have the option to apply your smartphone to deliver messages that are nice for your spouse. What matters is nurturing love and getting lovers of one another.

Perform around

Engage your spouse in many matches and behave like you were small children. Do not allow the years to prevent you from being a kid in your heart. If you've forgotten all your youth games, then research online, and you will discover more than enough matches. Playing not just brings you near another, but also includes a range of health benefits.

Be Affectionate

Never yell at your spouse when conveying. Always make sure you're close to them speak most beautifully. Play your loving nature and create your spouse feel as if they have an incredible impact on you personally, which is a turn-on.

Besides, once you're outside in people, hold on to your partner's armor snake that your hands about their mid areas as you wander along.

26

Thank Your Spouse

As soon as your spouse does something considerate, you owe them a "Thank you!" Accepting favors out of your spouse and neglecting to say "Thank you" is uncouth behavior.

Forgive Your Spouse

Ruthless individuals with stone-like hearts end up alone or at a certain lockup. But because you're not a callous individual, you wish to present your partner another opportunity if they flop. As important will be to maintain them in check.

Send Flowers

Cliché, yes, however, blossoms never run from fashion. Make sure that you're sending flowers to a significant other's area of work on your routine. Tuck naughty messages to the blossoms for your spouse comes home from the evening needing a "fight."

Prepare Their Favorite Meal

Food is a significant thing. If you're caring for his belly, he is very likely to grow fond of you. Fix his favorite meal now and again, and he will be forever grateful.

Be Wild in Bed

Do not be afraid to test new fashions or do things your lewd imagination indicates. Gender is just one of the locations that require constant development. When you adhere to a particular routine, your partner will know all of the tricks on your pockets, and they'll despise you for everything you have become. Thus, keep the eyes on the newest tendencies to surprise your guy.

CHAPTER 3 - The Uncommunicative Partner

It is one issue when one partner in a relationship does not talk, but if both partners do not talk, it indicates the end of the romantic relationship may be close. If partners stop telling each other their needs and wants, the couple may have already given up on each other. The couple lacks adequate motivation to work things out, and they may be waiting for one person to say it is time we break up.

Fear of Communicating

At times, partners in a romantic relationship may not talk because they feel that it will make things more damaging if they talk about the relationship. These couples still love each other, but they may not understand how to handle difficult subjects without damaging their relationship. Without them talking about the issues, or even the neutral feelings and thoughts, they start to lose their bond. Your interest in your loved one most likely developed out of talking about matters you both liked to talk about. Once you do not have them anymore, you may lose interest.

Barriers to Relationship Communication

There are various blocks to communication, and these barriers can be very destructive to your romantic relationship. Communication plays a very essential in connecting with your partner being open to your partner. To have a perfect conversation with your partner, you must have mutual respect essential in a loving relationship.

Barriers often interfere with the meaning of the message being communicated. These barriers lead to misunderstandings and pass unintentional information. Some conversation is more susceptible, like emotional arguments. Message barriers are prevalent if a person is in disagreement. During a misunderstanding, defenses inhibit your focus on what your partner is talking about. Inadequate focus leads to low listening techniques and frequent arguing. Even though feuds are the primary communication barriers, it is only one form of many you will identify in conversations.

Forms of Communication Blocks

Various blocks lead to disagreement. Most people are not aware of how their active listening techniques destroy conversations. Overcoming barriers can assist your love relationship as well as other bonds in your life.

Below are various conversational barriers that might be present:

Physical

It could be tough to get a perfect conversation if you got physical objects in your path. The distance can be a problem too when the person cannot hear you. The perfect way to talk to a person is to stand or sit across from their position. Distractions are another physical barrier. If possible, ensure that there are no distractions or interruptions during discussions.

Misperception

At times while talking to your partner, one misperceives what the other partner is talking about. This occurs when you think your partner is angry over one issue but is furious about another issue. This misunderstanding can cause bad advice or feedback that can make the person feel ignored. When you ever feel that you have a misplaced perception, try to ask the person for clarity.

Psychological Interference

It is a popular block and can be hard to run away from. Emotional stress can interfere with attentive listening. When you are having a difficult day or going through very personal issues, it is hard to focus on what other people are talking about. If this is an issue, you will require your partner to know that it is not the appropriate moment, but you would want to talk about it after.

Inadequate Experience

Sometimes in a romantic relationship, partners do not have the same life experiences. If this happens, one partner will have a difficult time focusing or following. To be an attentive listener, you must ask your partner for clarity where you do not understand and be patient while you attempt to follow.

Not Listening

You require to desire to listen. When you do not feel that you can listen attentively to your partner, you require your partner to know that you cannot focus at that particular moment. Neglecting what your partner says ignites resentment and anger. Allowing your partner to know that you cannot listen attentively is because you are busy will prevent hard feelings between you two.

Unsolicited Advice

Most people love to vent and not receive advice. When you desire to give advice, it can damage the conversation you are having with your significant other. Unsolicited advice prevents others from being open. Encourage and allow him/her to know that you are there if required. Your significant other will ask for advice if he/she wants one.

Language and Cultural

Cultural and language differences exist in the manner in which partners talk to each other. You may figure out that most people will stand too close to you while others stand further away. Most cultures will not allow you to look at your partner while talking because it appears to send the wrong information. Knowing the cultures can assist your significant other, and you deal with poor communication. Language and the definition of words can be an issue because of misunderstandings, even if you speak a similar language.

Nonverbal Cues

Your nonverbal signs are just as essential as your verbal language. What you are saying has to match what you are performing. When you say that you are actively listening, but you are looking the other way, you send a mixed message. Most people will halt talking if they feel that you are not paying close attention, even when you tell them you are actively listening. Pay close attention to your physical expression as well as your words when speaking with your love partner.

How to Avoid Blocks in a Relationship?

Attentive listening is the perfect technique to avoid barriers in communication. As your significant other is speaking, ask relevant questions to clarify without distracting. If your significant other has finished speaking, acknowledge that you were listening attentively by saying, "I know how hard this must be for you." Your significant other will appreciate that you heard the concerns and you are concerned and empathetic.

Learning how to communicate with your significant other healthily can significantly enhance your relationship. Being patient with yourself as you learn these techniques and knowledge takes time for these new communication skills to stick.

Understanding Yourself

To communicate with your significant other appropriately, you will first require to understand your needs. Think about how you process information and how you express your thoughts to those around you.

Internal Processing

When you are an internal processor, you like to take your time and think about your reactions before responding to someone. You may even rehearse what you have to say aloud or in your mind before saying anything. Others may speak over you or get frustrated with your reaction time. Allowing your significant other to know how your process information can assist them better understand how to communicate to you.

External Processing

When you are an external processor, you like to talk through things aloud. You may necessarily require a response as you work through what you are trying to say.

Recognizing Your Emotions

Before you start speaking with your significant other, check-in with yourself, do a tight body check, and see if any part is carrying any tension or anxiety. After that, identify what feelings are coming up for you. Connecting with your body can help you recognize your feelings and the intensity better to articulate your emotions to your significant other appropriately.

I Statements

I statements let you tell you are significant other what is happening with you emotionally without blaming them. This builds a more receptive environment for your significant other. For you to create an "I" statement:

- Identifying what feelings are coming up for you

- Identifying what stimulated your response

- Apply the template: "I feel (insert feeling) when this (insert situation occurs).'

Listening Respectfully

It can be difficult not to start thinking of a reaction when a person begins speaking, particularly in a heated conversation. To completely participate with your significant other, apply attentive listening techniques.

Clarify Statements

When you are not clear about your significant other, it is essential to ask. Keep in mind that asking questions can help you work through whatever issue you are talking about together.

Connecting with Your Significant Other

Healthy communication techniques are part of having a caring, loving, and sincere relationship. Both your significant other and you can work on these skills together and enhance your social skills together.

CHAPTER 4 - Principles for Dealing with Conflict

We all live and work with people, but everyone is different. And it's even more difficult if you are a businessman, the boss. You don't just work with people; you also work with people who work with people who work with people. As a leader, you are answerable for the outcomes and still have to get people to succeed and work together. Human relations are inevitably complex and contradictory.

All good leaders will finally learn some crucial lessons from dispute resolution. There aren't many of them —only around eight. But if you do not know these eight essential concepts and apply them, human problems will make your leadership chaotic, and your life is exhausting. It is, therefore, necessary to learn the eight principles —three criteria and five steps.

The Fundamental Principles of Highly Effective Conflict Resolution

A leader must have a strategy in his or her organization for coping with conflict. Leaders must overcome conflicts at the source by improving relationships and better knowing both sides of the dispute's desires.

Adopt The Right Mindset

When they face confrontation, most people do a lot of wrong things. For example, they typically avoid conflicts at almost every cost and often take care of their hurts for a long time before they talk to another, often talk about a conflict with other people instead of the one who can truly solve the problem and sometimes chat or criticize them for trying to feel better about themselves and the situation.

When they attempt to converse with the other person in dispute, they often want to take the easy route by leaving a message online, a speech, or send a letter. In reality, these forms of avoidance cause more problems.

All these errors, and others like them, are confusing, and small problems or misunderstandings can lead to severe problems.

Top leaders prevent such failures when they take the correct view.

Precondition 1

Address the responsible party explicitly and promptly instead of damage.

Speak to the person who hurt you if others have hurt you. Explicitly. Explicitly. Don't wait. Don't wait. Do it immediately.

Orrin Woodward referenced this significant subject in his discourse named "Compromise– Relationships forever:

"Contention resembles a fire. Easy to snuff out in the event that it is little yet practically unmanageable on the off chance that it isn't dealt with without any problem. Envision hitting the sack around evening time and taking a gander at your room corner, and seeing a little fire sprinkling out. You want to fail to remember it and hit the sack, realizing that in the first part of the day you'll converse with it. In the event that you like your home, this is presumably not a smart thought. What's more, it is anything but a sensible arrangement to straightforwardly address the issue in the event that you need to keep up great relations and progress.

Frequently, it's convoluted, yet it tends to be summed up as follows how veritable pioneers respond to struggle or even potential clashes:

- Explain would requirements be able to have not been satisfied.

- Brainstorm and give the other individual the best aims.

- Explicitly approach the other individual and address that person.

- Using the accompanying five measures

- Do the entirety of this legitimately, with no mischief or disdain.

This is the first and fundamental precondition: manage questions quickly by direct correspondence with different gatherings.

Precondition 2

Address the opposite side instead of tattle.

All around numerous individuals who feel hurt quit talking straightforwardly to the next individual. All things being equal, they address a ton of others. This is tattle. This is tattle. This is an investigation as well. What's more, they are both the foes of initiative and accomplishment.

Clashes will happen, individuals will be, and there will be mistaken assumptions, harms and broken desires, and different debates. Individuals know about this and are making arrangements for it. Specifically, whenever hurt or contradiction occurs, they make a move by:

- Explaining what guidelines have not been met.

- Giving the other individual the best expectations

- Do not reason fears, mishaps, or other unfavorable impacts to get more prominent

- Never chuckle or false the opposite side.

- Approaching someone else to fix issues straightforwardly and with affection (utilizing five stages)

- Doing this straight away without permitting negative emotions time to create.

- This is the way to administration, the dependable method to react to struggle.

Precondition 3

Defy questions as opposed to depend on electronic correspondences

In any event, when individuals take the right viewpoint, they commit the error of certainly communicating contradictions and antagonistic occasions. This is ordinarily done through email, voice, or web-based media. The issue is that any non-intuitive contact seems to strengthen –not perfect– the fire of contention.

At whatever point you have something terrible to share, essentially when managing a debate, do so eye to eye, if conceivable, and at any rate face to face on the telephone (or utilizing one of the numerous the present video talk alternatives). Never utilize non-intelligent organizations to attempt to settle the contest. On the off chance that you need to send an email or leave a message, basically be idealistic and told the individual you'd love to address them and welcome their call. At that point, speak with them legitimately face to face.

The more noteworthy the negative, harmed, or contradiction real or future, the more you need to cooperate for a superior arrangement. Does it face to face if the contest is serious or capably enthusiastic? Never endeavor to settle the contest by text, online media, or voice message.

The Steps of Effective Conflict Resolution

Presently, when we take the correct point of view, it's an ideal opportunity to talk around five stages. Make a move if there is a difference between you or any other person.

Step 1 – Affirm The Relationship

The proportions of profoundly effective compromise are clear and direct with the right mentality. Stage 1 is companionship approval. Kick back and state to the next gathering: "I may be awkward, however, I'm here on the grounds that I regard our companionship considerably more than my solace and data."

Let me know, "I'm certain there was a slip-up, and I need to realize how I ought to have improved, and afterward take care of business."

Do this in a feeling of empathy, warmth, and certifiable assurance to rise above any distinctions. This is the initial step.

At the beginning of any contest goal, it is basically important. Conceivably the full goal will implode on the off chance that you attempt to skirt this stage. It's so essential and strong.

Step 2 – Genuinely Seek for Understanding

On the off chance that you approve the relationship to the degree where others feel more complete on their financial balance and can work, the accompanying advance is to comprehend. Try not to start by guaranteeing the other party gets you; first, focus on the other party's agreement.

What were the desires not satisfied for her? What befell this misconception? What was the deal? (Regularly, what you believe was occurring and what was going on isn't the equivalent.) What was she thinking? What was she thinking? Since what did she think?

There are urgent things to comprehend and mostly to clarify what has occurred. This will wipe out a few errors. Be that as it may, with these immediate inquiries, it is important not simply to pester the other individual. Let her depict them in her terms, instead of in her language. Listen cautiously. A great many people aren't extremely effective; however, pioneers need to make it a top ability. Tune in.

The key to listening effectiveness is the mirror impact, which gives us the method of mirrors. This implies that you speak to what the other individual says to you. It's moderately simple; it's only one point you make. Top pioneers realize it's an absolute necessity. Ordinarily, you won't encounter any effective contest goal on the off chance that you don't do this.

The look is amazingly strong. It tells the other person that you listen, and it also tells you that you listen. Mirroring keeps you focused on what the other person does and what you need, want, and feel. If you're not voicing words from other people, you're not listening either. Because if you don't listen to the person, you don't feel listened to, you don't fix anything.

People need to be heard, and they should feel understood when they do. Only then will they be mentally able to think about concrete solutions. If you want to settle a problem, you just have to try to grasp it first. Listen carefully and use the Mirror Technique repeatedly until the other person tells you heard him entirely.

Step 3 – Lovingly Seek to Be Understood

The most important term here is loving! If you don't like your answers, you usually fall on deaf ears. How your messages sometimes feel is more important than the actual words you use. When you lovingly share your thoughts and feelings about the situation, note that the resolution is your goal. The aim is to clarify how you didn't feel about what the other party should have done.

Step 3 is necessary even though step 1 and step 2 fix several misunderstandings and hurt feelings. Another person wants good emotions from the fact that he knew what was happening. Then, talk about the issues –he needs to hear from your viewpoint and shares your views about the dispute, so you can avoid letting residual emotions develop and become stronger.

It is imperative not to make a common yet hurtful mistake as the conversation continues. Do not give the other individual reasons or speak in an attack. For instance, say, "You didn't call, and I felt," but don't say," You didn't call intentionally, that made me feel like that."

Both the motivation and blame are accusatory and angry, and the listener is inclined to feel and respond defensively. Please share your experience and how it made you feel, not comment on another person's feelings, actions, or activities.

When both parties have expressed their views and concerns freely and lovingly, and both feel respected and understood, there can be a genuine and substantive resolution of a dispute. Both parties may have healthier relationships and connections than before the dispute.

Step 4 – Own the Responsibility and Sincerely Apologize

"True leaders pursue ways to be transparent while protecting the other party's ego. It yields two to tango and two to fail. None of us is perfect, so you can always take some responsibility for it if there is a disagreement. Even if you are not sure that there was a disagreement, you may take the responsibility not to communicate more clearly and know how someone else feels.

Your words should be genuine and honest, but start taking responsibility when you see anything you can do better. Don't hold those stuff in your mouth. Vocalize it freely and say you're sorry. In so doing, you show that you do your best, all you can to solve the situation and restore the full sense of friendship and cooperation. It's strong.

CHAPTER 5 - Empathic Speaking Skill

The Question: "How can I say what I want to say in a way that accurately expresses my thoughts and feelings, and at the same time increases the likelihood the other person will be open to hear and receive it, whether it's a pleasant and agreeable topic or something we disagree on, or even something I'm upset about?"

Empathic Speaking Skill Has Five Steps

Step 1: Clarify and Organize Your Thoughts Before You Speak. "If You Blurt, You Could Hurt!"

This is a big one. How many times have you yelled out some hurtful words when you were upset only to feel within seconds that it was an insensitive, damaging thing to do? In my classes, I'll ask that same question, "How many of you have blurted out some angry words in the heat of the moment, totally blasting the other person, only to feel bad about it soon after?" Nearly everyone raises their hand. It may have been a cathartic emotional release at the moment, but the fallout was usually negative. Suppose we can just hit the "pause" button for a second, gather ourselves, recognize our feelings, and more thoughtfully choose the words and tone of voice that expresses our concerns. In that case, we will be much more likely to have our concerns heard and received by the other person—which is our goal anyway.

If you blurt out angry, hurtful words with a harsh tone of voice, the listener will likely do one of three things, often referred to as the Fight, Flight, or Freeze Response:

1.   Fight: Lash back at you with the same kind of angry language, in which case the argument escalates and can even spin out of control; or

2.   Flight (Flee): Get very defensive, withdraw and shut down, and throw up a wall of silence because they don't want to get stung or make matters worse; or

3.   Freeze: Be stunned, shocked, and unsure how to feel or react. Frozen in a location like a deer caught in the headlights.

None of these scenarios is helpful, and none of them result in what you're hoping for, which is to express your concerns and feelings and receive an understanding, empathic response from the person you're speaking to.

If you simply blow off steam and your words and mannerisms hurt others, especially the people you love and thought about, though it may be a cathartic, emotional release for you, it can create a lot of immediate and long-term relationship damage. Think before you speak—how it will come out and how it will be received.

"I-Statements" vs. "You-Statements"

Here's an effective method for expressing your thoughts and feelings in a non-inflammatory way: Prepare to speak in "I-Statements," such as, "I think…", "I feel…", "I want…", "I would like…", "I'm concerned…", etc.

I-Statements show that your statements come from you—your thoughts, feelings, and concerns—and are much easier for the listener to receive and respond to than finger-pointing, accusatory You-Statements, which are often expressed and received as flames. The listener will react against those negative expressions because they don't want to get burned.

Examples of "You-Statements" restated as "I-Statements":

- "You're way too loud!" can be restated,

"I would like you to please lower your voice."

- "You never listen to me!" can be restated,

"I want you to listen to me when I'm speaking to you."

- "You make me so angry!" can be restated,

"I feel distraught when you..."

Notice that using I-Statements can express your concerns and desires clearly but not in an attacking or accusatory way, thus making it more likely you'll receive less resistance from the listener to what you're saying or requesting than had you expressed yourself with a more aggressive You-Statement. Of course, you can't control the other person's response, but you can make it a bit easier for them to respond in the ways you're hoping for.

Step 2: Express with Respect. Choose Your Words Well, And Be Aware of Your Tone of Voice. Be Sensitive to The Heart of The Person You're Speaking To—If You Do, They'll Be More Likely to Listen

This is a close add-on to Step 1—how you say what you want to say.

In one of my men's classes in jail, an inmate said, "I don't understand my wife. She wasn't saying much, and I tried to get her to tell me what was wrong, and she wouldn't tell me."

I asked, "What did you say to her?" He said, "How come you're stomping around the house, acting like such a bitch?"

The class burst out in laughter, but he was serious. I looked at him and said, "Hmm, I think I see the problem. If you were to put yourself in her shoes, and she said to you, 'How come you're stomping around the house acting like such a jerk?' how would you feel?" "Pretty angry," he said. "Exactly, you'd feel disrespected.

That's probably how she felt. Now let's observe if we can come up with something she might be open to hearing."

We then worked out a better way to say it, something like, "You seem upset. Is there something wrong?" and then I told him to listen to her with an open mind to hear what she had to say. This is an extreme example, but illustrative. There's a big difference between, "Why are you acting like such a bitch?" and "What's wrong?"

The reality is that if someone speaks to us disrespectfully, we have no incentive to respond favorably to their concerns or requests and give them the impression that it's okay for them to talk to us like that—even if they're right. Why reward or encourage that kind of mistreatment? If someone speaks to us disrespectfully, we may holler and push back or shut down entirely like this inmate's wife did. Again, you reap what you sow. Sow disrespect, and it will bounce back at you. Sow respect, and there's a greater chance that respect will be returned. We can determine what happens by what comes out of our mouths.

I like this quote by Dr. Frank Luntz: "It's not what you say; it's what people hear." Even if you say the right words, but you say them with a disrespectful tone and attitude, the other person will hear the disrespect and not your words.

Especially when you're upset, it's important to express with respect. Remember, this is a fellow human being you're talking to. Treat them as you would like to be treated.

Step 3: Express Your Points Clearly, What You Want or Need, What You Feel. Don't Be Vague. Don't Expect the Other Person to Read Your Mind. Speak about One Issue at a Time

If you're married or in a pledged relationship, you may have said or heard this one before: "If you loved me, you'd know what I want." If we guess what we want, a requirement of whether a person loves us or not, they may not guess correctly. It doesn't mean they don't love or care for us, because they do; it merely means they can't tell everything that's going on inside of us. Better that we spell it out—make it clear.

For example, if you want to go out on a dinner date with your spouse or partner, instead of waiting for them to intuit your desire somehow, it's better to spell it out, say what you want. "I'd like to go out on a date together. Can we go out to dinner tonight?" Your message is clear. The vaguer you are with what you want or need, or what you feel, the more likely the listener will not respond in the ways you would like. It helps them to help you if you express your points to them clearly.

Also, speak about one issue or concern at a time. Don't jump from one thing to another, or you may confuse and overwhelm the listener. And be careful not to speak too long on any given point, or you might lose the listener's attention. Your goal is to be heard and understood by the listener. Make it easy for them to do so.

Step 4: Pause for the Listener's Response. If They Don't Say Anything after You've Spoken, You Might Ask, "What Did You Understand about What I Said?" Or "I'm Interested to Know What You Think and Feel about What I Said." Then Listen to Their Response

Again, the more critical, severe, or emotion-filled the topic, the more vital it is to communicate clearly and then give the other person a chance to respond. Ideally, they will know how to do Empathic Listening and say back in their own words the main points they heard you say and the feelings they sensed in you, and then express their thoughts and feelings on the subject. But even if they don't know these communication skills, you can invite them to respond.

Either way, pausing for their response lets them know you are interested in knowing what they heard, if they have any questions or what they feel about the subject. This helps avoid any misunderstandings between the two of you now or after regarding this critical matter.

Step 5: Thank Them for Listening to You. You Can Simply Say, "Thanks for Listening"

If the person has heard you out and invested their time and energy to do so, it's important to appreciate them for it. A simple "Thank you" lets them know their listening was essential to you, affirms them for it, and encourages them to continue to be good listeners in the future. Don't take their listening for granted—thank them for it. They'll appreciate being appreciated.

CHAPTER 6 - Communicating When Angry

One of the few things that makes communication difficult is when you allow your anger to get in the way of your conversations. You must eliminate your anger issues first to create and maintain a healthy relationship when you have a conversation.

They do not know what you would like unless you tell them. But the question is, how do you tell them what you need? Do you say it with anger? If you do, then the chances are that their response will determine the whole conversation's direction. It gets worse if they respond defensively or angrily.

An important point to note is that communicating without anger takes a lot of self-awareness most people lack. People's most common mistake is exploding and saying hurtful words they will wish they could take back. Even though your spouse did something that was entirely out of line, choosing to communicate without anger goes a long way in getting things cleared up fast so that you avoid resentment.

Let's face it; being in an intimate relationship, much less a marriage, is not easy. Ensuring that you and your spouse have everything you need takes a lot of openness, honesty, and zero blame games. You are both humans who are far from perfect! You cannot always put your partner first if you are bogged down by life's circumstances that you allow to spin out of control. The same thing goes for your partner.

Now, let us ponder a situation where you are upset about your spouse's behavior. What do you do? You start overthinking and ruminating over the whole situation. You allow the tape of your conversation to play in your mind over and over again. You keep revisiting who did what and who said what.

Before long, you curve your spouse into a monster, something that he is not. You fell in love with him, and the chances are that he is nothing like a monster; otherwise, why would you be with him in the first place?

You simply have to recognize that your spouse is probably trying hard to meet his obligations so that you both can be happy together. In the meantime, you feel as though you have been put on the back burner, ignored and mistreated. Yes, this feeling is not good, but the question is, are you familiar with the whole situation?

When something similar occurs, communicating with anger and yelling at your spouse is likely to happen. You probably will start saying hurtful things that you cannot take back. What you are merely doing is making the whole situation worse than it already is. You will push him away and what happens is that he will wall off and not feel heard at all.

One thing that I have noticed when this happens is that you start convincing yourself that it is not so big of a deal. However, the truth is that you cannot let it go, and it starts eating into your relationship bits by bits until what is left of it is resentment and unprocessed issues.

But what if you choose to be clear, centered, and emotionally aware of what is going on? Well, the truth is simply will be better placed to handle the whole situation with an open heart, faith, and so much grace.

You first need to discover what your core needs are when you are upset. Realize that your emotions at that point are like waves; they come and go away. However, beneath these waves of emotions is essential information. The question is, where do they end up?

It is important to note that if you fail to process these emotions or even recognize that they exist, you will be repressing them. Each time you fight with your spouse, you bottle it in, and sooner than you think, it all explodes.

You cannot be walking around with that much body weight. This is too much emotional weight that you need to let go of. Well, I will not tell you how to lighten that load, but I will certainly help you stay on the clear from what is upsetting you. This way, you can virtually communicate with your spouse and the people in your life without anger, giving you a better chance of ensuring that all of your needs in marriage are met.

You cannot change your spouse's frustrating behavior. However, what you can do is let him know in a more centered way how his/her behavior affects you. No one likes hurting their loved ones intentionally; at least, that is how I like to see it. Most of the mistakes we make are unconscious and do not have ill intentions.

Therefore, it is up to you to ensure that you let your spouse know what you need and want from them. Throwing tantrums, pretending to be okay when you are not, and shutting down your emotions will not solve anything. It will only poison your marriage more and more each day.

To keep that connection between you and your spouse, you have to learn how to communicate with them without anger effectively. To accomplish this, you have first to determine what your core needs are when trapped in an upsetting situation. Once you have that, know, then it is time that you have to learn how to give that need a clear and heart-centered voice.

How do you do that?

It would be best to process these emotions before communicating with your partner to know your core needs. Rather than exploding in healthy anger when talking to your spouse, these steps are going to help you put things under control. You will not have to avoid the whole situation or suck up.

Yes, your anger is valid, but you have to take care of yourself emotionally. This is not your spouse's job.

CHAPTER 7 - Unproductive Argumentation

If you're dating or in a particular partnership, you've unquestionably discovered that several of the disputes in your relationship never appear to be settled. Instead, they get reprocessed. Why does it happen too often? So why not sound insoluble under such situations? Precise reasons for this include: It is a perfect way to defend your pride when under siege to get upset with your spouse and spouse. So it will become routine to go crazy as an almost feasible way to defend your susceptibility, which we have so little knowledge of. And if you realize that your companion's acts make you feel pretty uncomfortable at a primitive level, you will be inspired to assault physically (or neutralize-attack) them. Amusingly, when your companion's inconsistencies cause you sadness, or whether you feel threatened by them, violent reactions quickly stave off the anxiety that is beginning to emerge from the very core of your being. So we should only be looking ahead to enjoying ourselves. If someone else asks about our integrity, morals, intelligence, so those optimistic feelings will easily sound threatened by themselves. You would be compelled to fend off any potential danger or indignity immediately before you are fully self-validating, such that you are not taken too close to the heart from another's negative opinion. You're allowed to break under the belt in these cases, sometimes well below the belt. Hence, you accuse the partner of whatever sort about the nastiness that you might think about, harshly apply the toughest, rudely threaten them, most objectionable motives to them, strike them with a preferred mark, ride the morally more superior "greater-horse" and offer them (uninvited) a wholly unappealing diagnosis of behavior, pompously lecturing them on their workaround. Additionally, while you're battling another person (most likely your spouse, since it's generally the most vulnerable connection), you're afflicted with the stress reaction known as "fight or flight." Hence, this stressed condition's whole-body readiness produces dopamine, strengthens you mentally, and gives you a feeling of strength and influence that might have been unbearable just seconds ago. This will offer you a strong understanding of how unnecessarily impressive outrage can be, with its peculiar power to hold debilitating self-doubts bursting from culture. The trouble with annoyance is that it keeps you from actually listening to your companion's complaints, which may be genuine and deserve the utmost attention. Possibly, if you argue with both, you can bet that neither of you can ever listen closely to the others. And that's crucial to what anger accomplishes, it lets you move free from an anxiety-producing learning atmosphere, and you're entirely concentrating on marshaling the truth against your clear-in-the-wrong partner.

What can be the solution?

What's needed here is to strengthen your faith and understand how to defend yourself. Know that your friend's decision affects them as often as it concerns you in certain situations. Hence you alone assert the freedom to judge yourself, but you can do so gently with respect, compassion, even approval. And so you don't need to rely on anger any more to defend yourself from someone's cruel judgment. Notice also that the nervous, anxious brain component will regulate you before you can settle down. Suppose your marital difficulties are to be successfully overcome. In that case, you can need to layaway your valid opinion and focus on your spouse's opposing point of view and do so with reverence and consideration. So identifying with your mate's position will alleviate much of your anger itself, so admiring the abstract worth even when you find it not similar to your own.

Your parents warned you that it was not easy to overcome conflict.

Accidentally though, you were attempting to exchange partner points with your caregivers, and that's precisely what they were doing. If they differed, they would both dig in their heels and claim the superiority of their position steadfastly and self-righteously, rather than pretending to understand each other's point of view in a way that might contribute to mutually beneficial compromise. And hold marital harmony back then.

In brief, they were terrible models to teach you how to handle your childhood social discords. Their willingness, or influence, to engage in dispute constructively was zero. And the incompatible fights between intimate companions are all you finally took away from their fights. On the contrary, as your internal pressure cooker began rising, what you could do was blast up and read up the riot act to your companion. And unfortunately, the only way to relieve your frustration from such a response would be to leave your companion so embarrassed by your rage that they simply revoked you. Such coerced submission will only bring further damage to any romantic bond that remains between you.

It is safe to assume, in these cases, that your parents ignored the problem-solving skills of ordinary individuals. Both spouses will firmly stop the discussions in a stand-off or go deaf, throwing up an unscalable, unbreachable shield against further dialogue. Finally, they are too exhausted or frustrated to begin arguing for issues that they are no closer to fixing than before they started.

What can be the solution?

First of all, question yourself that do you do any of the counterproductive stuff? In the act of brainlessly modeling what your parents would regularly display right before your eyes when you get upset, will you capture yourself? If you push the keys, you can react automatically. So what's expected here is to obey how your parents did when they were upset, which means an unconscious part here.

If you've imitated their habits as a child, these responses will also be instilled or programmed within you. And sadly, when you feel frustrated, they will be at hand, and they're going to sound convenient for you to run. That's precisely what you need to reconfigure, and it all starts with both information and "a-where-ness," but you're going to have to figure it out right when you get triggered. More specifically, you'll need to build a mentality that reconciles much of your disputes with each other. It's axiomatic that successful partnerships are built on compromise. So when you figure a way to fulfill one another's contradictory needs, equilibrium will be established among the two of you.

There are specific fundamental gaps between you two, perhaps attributable to your philosophies or your natures, and they obviously cannot be resolved.

Therefore, the situation accounts for the prolonged stalemates. These irresolvable contradictions may be accustomed, consented to, or modified; however, they cannot be reversed or made compatible. Suppose your partner's extroversion always triggers your nerves as they want to go out to do something when you're essentially a personality can be called an introvert, a home person, able to pursue your interests happily putter around the home on your own. In that case, your partner may well answer, what is wrong with you? Anything you will never like to hear. In exchange, you may be made to gripe, why do we have to go every time? What is wrong with just getting the kids and me sitting at home? Aren't we enough for you?

Dependent on your physiology, you'll either need more or less superior stimulation than the rest. It is something you obviously can't manage, and moaning about it relates more to anyone of you worrying about how your partner invalidates who you are, too. If you start to think about it, this is kind of insane or at least mad-making. You don't care about morality or vices but inquire about human predispositions. Since you have a marked preference for sweets, it's not fair to object to your spouse's urge for, if one says, chocolate ice cream. However, maybe irrationally, we all feel bothered by these unchanging discords.

What can be the solution?

The option to lock such a relationship on the grid will be clear. Suppose there are items that you and your spouse will never really settle about. In that case, it is best to remove them from your conversation until such time as one of you is deliberately reassessing principles that you once felt absolute. But no matter actually how open-minded you could be on other stuff, it's still likely you've decided on those topics. And the spouses have the exact, sadly. And if you both are close-minded, both of you must consider these are not changing differences and embrace them.

Notice that, before now, you can eliminate all that has caused you so much unnecessary pain when you continue to accept those discomfiting facets of the maquillage or acquired principles of your spouse. Say to yourself: What choice is this? That puts some distance between you both to look at your partner for views that oppose you. But the loneliness could interfere with the urge, or tendency, to communicate in person with them.

CHAPTER 8 - Difficulties with Resolving Conflicts and Problems

The reason why we are often returning to conflicts and disagreements, and ways to resolve these problems, lies in the fact that many couples are struggling with negative communication in terms of being unable to effectively and efficiently resolve their disagreements. The key to resolving negative communication is establishing equality in the relationship and focusing on understanding your partner's point of view rather than brainstorming on how to defend your ego from being attacked by your partner. When you decide to give trust and receive trust, you also need to be ready to understand that giving trust means that you will also have confidence in the fact that your partner is not trying to attack you just for the sake of making you feel bad. In case both partners are aware that there is a problem that needs to be solved and consider the possibility that they are responsible for the problem, it will be easier to resolve conflicts and disagreements.

Accepting that your partner's dissatisfaction is not attacking you but instead challenged to work together with your partner towards solving your problems creates a healthy environment where both partners can express themselves. Communication in relationships is one of the critical components of a healthy relationship and connection between you and your partner, which is why you should try to approach every conflict with calmness and readiness to communicate with your partner so you could solve the problem together. Inability to find an agreement and resolve conflicts may also create negative communication, which appears as a side effect of prolonged miscommunication. It may seem to both partners like everyday communication is no longer possible. Negative communication can be any form of communication that makes one or both partners feel depressed, discontent, insecure, hurt, and offended.

As earlier mentioned, communication in relationships is not only limited to verbal communication - instead, your tone of voice matters, as well as your body language and facial expressions. To escape the zone of negative conformism where negative communication has become an everyday asset that the couple uses as a standard way of communicating, you need to make an effort. That effort can include a daily routine where you and your partner will share your thoughts and daily experiences, i.e., how was work, how was your day, did something happen, etc. You can agree on having dinner together or having a morning coffee together, so you would be given more room for openly communicating with your partner positively.

Poor Sex Life

Can a couple grow tired of each other in bed? The answer is probably. In case you and your partner are failing at making an effort to show your partner that you are attracted to them and that you care, your sex life may be suffering. Many studies conducted on couples indicate that dissatisfactory sex life is one of the main problems people encounter in relationships, causing a breakup after causing a loss of connection, intimacy, and passion. You and your partner may feel the lack of chemistry and attraction between you, which may appear due to being together for a long time in a relationship with low dynamics. Once you stop trying to make your relationship work as it used to, it is the point where problems may appear.

One of these problems is losing the feeling of being attracted to your partner, which may lead to infidelity and break up if the problem is not resolved and your relationship improved. Feeling attractive to your partner and being attracted to your partner is essential for keeping your relationship dynamics up, which means that you need to remind yourself of what made you attracted to your partner in the first place. You want to evoke all the good stuff and avoid thinking about other things such as problems at work or struggling with finances, which are some of the most commonly noted problems that may cause a lack of libido. Inability to solve these problems and similar issues may seriously affect your and your partner's libido, making you unable to think about sex and attraction when you are stressing out around existential problems.

You shouldn't allow external factors such as stress to affect this part of intimacy with your partner. Learn each other's sexual needs as if you are intimate for the first time –this case should help you revoke the passion you once had. Don't be afraid to express your needs regarding sex, while you and your partner could also experiment with new poses as long as both of you feel comfortable with experimenting. Set up a date night that will end in your bed, and try to awake attraction that most certainly exists between you as long as you are ready to make an effort for the sake of happiness in your relationship.

Inability to Comply with Changes in Your Relationship

We are all inclined towards constant and periodic changes, while changes in changing life stages represent perfectly normal progress in anyone's life. Sometimes, as we change, the way we observe others and relationships with other people likewise changes. During our personal development and individual changes, our partners' changes co-occur. In contrast, it may occur that the way we changed doesn't match the idea of change noted in our partner's metamorphosis. Although you are both still the same people, you can notice that your necessities are changing as your relationship is developing, which may bring issues to your relationship if you and your partner cannot comply with these changes. Any change may positively or negatively affect your relationship, starting from changing your job and profession to deciding that your relationship is ready to take off to the following stage. Inability to reply to these changes positively may create disagreements between you and your partner, while you may also feel that you have outgrown each other.

Allowing External Factors to Affect Your Relationship

We are all vulnerable to external factors and outside stressors at times or frequently. We manage multiple essential aspects of our life – job, kids, home, finances, friends, family, and relationship with our partners. Not all these aspects will appear to be functional when we become more vulnerable to external stress factors. While life may create many scenarios that can put you in distress, your relationship shouldn't be affected by these factors if you have a strong base in your relationship. Suppose you and your partner are not investing enough energy and effort into keeping your relationship going upwards. In that case, it is more likely that external negative factors will have adverse effects on your relationship, affecting both you and your partner. In cases where a couple allows external factors to get in the way of their relationship, the relationship between them may come crumbling down, leading to conflicts, stress, misunderstandings, and disagreements. In this case, you also need to note that every relationship has ups and downs, which is a perfectly normal thing.

In contrast, a relationship's strength can be measured by a couple's ability to overcome difficulties and make their relationship more robust, even in the most challenging times. If you love, respect, and appreciate each other, you will be able to share your fears and doubts with your partner to resolve your problems together. Stressful things WILL happen to both of you –sometimes simultaneously, while you may feel lonely in your distress on different occasions. What is essential is not to allow these stressful experiences to affect the relationship between you and your partner —to learn how to stay immune to distress when it comes to preserving your relationship, you need to adopt a supportive attitude, where you and your partner will be working together to overcome problems that you may encounter in the form of external damaging factors.

Infidelity and Betrayal

Hopefully, not a common problem in relationships, but infidelity counts as one of the significant betrayal forms with the ability to shake up even the most vital foundations found in relationships. Whether it is about seeking acceptance and approval elsewhere or trying to find passion and physical satisfaction with someone else other than your partner, motifs for cheating on your partner may be different, while the result may always be the same: someone ends up hurt and betrays. It is difficult to move on with sharing a relationship after an act of infidelity as some of the critical qualities of a healthy relationship have been compromised. Trust, honesty, support, intimacy, connection —all these qualities may fall under the negative influence of infidelity, directly disturbing the foundation of your relationship. Although considered a "cardinal sin" for relationship commandments, consequences from infidelity and betrayal can be worked through if the couple is ready to forgive and accept that people change for better and worse likewise. If both partners agree that infidelity can be forgiven, the couple may continue working on retrieving trust and practicing honesty. The first step is to locate and confess what made you or your partner turn to infidelity while staying in a relationship. Was it the lack of affection? The lack of appreciation? Insecurity? Will it happen again?

Money and Finances

While not the most romantic thing globally, money and finances are a pain point in many relationships where a couple is married, engaged to be married, or living together. As a couple, you share many things, so money and finances and how the money is spent on an everyday basis might also be shared. For instance, if you live together with your partner, you will share your rent or pay the bills together, or agree to share the money you spend on food. You probably have shared finances and personal funds that you spend on your clothes, coffee, lunch break, etc. Even when finances are not shared, the mere pressure that comes with bills and financial obligations can affect a relationship between a financial crisis that one or both partners are struggling with. Stress is a common side effect that arrives with money problems, so once the financial problems kick in, the stress levels consequently hit the roof. In cases where finances are shared between a couple, one or both partners may blame each other in times of crisis, bringing more problems to the table and shakes up the relationship's foundation. It is essential to stay healthy and figure out what to do together, especially in times of crisis when cooperation, clear communication, trust, and support are all about to be tested. It is in times of crisis that the strength of a relationship is best tested.

CHAPTER 9 - Some Example of Conversation and Dialogue in Different Day Moments

What does a relationship defined by good communication look like? Here are eight habits that couples who communicate well practice all the time. We'll give examples of the habits in action when relevant:

They Express Their Appreciation for Each Other

Good communication is about staying in sync, not only about hard things and conflicts but also about positive feelings. Couples who communicate well are always showing their love and appreciation for each other. This can include thoughtful texts, little love notes, compliments, and friendly gestures. Even on busy days when distractions abound, an emotionally-healthy couple always remembers to show each other some love, even if it seems small. This habit nurtures the security of the relationship, and both people never feel underappreciated or neglected.

Examples:

Text your partner "I love you" in the morning, so it's the first thing they see when they wake up.

Bring your partner flowers, their favorite snack, or a movie when you know they've had a bad day.

When your significant other does something around the house like cooking dinner, doing the dishes, or putting the kids to bed, say, "Thank you."

Send your partner a song that makes you think of them.

Tell your partner, "You look outstanding today."

Learn your partner's love language, and work on expressing your feelings towards them in a way they connect with.

They Make Positivity a Priority

Studies support the idea that intentionally working on positive thinking and reducing negative self-talk can make a person happier. The same applies to relationships. Couples, who actively make an effort to say positive things, especially during arguments, are happier and enjoy healthier relationships. A relationship with lots of negative energy is bound to make one or both depressed, cynical, and frustrated. Instead of a source of happiness, the relationship becomes a source of stress. If the couple commits to being more positive, seeing the silver lining as much as possible, and expressing it out loud, both people get a boost and feel more secure.

They Physically Connect

The physical connection doesn't mean sex, though regular sex is often a sign of a healthy relationship. Besides that, other physical contact is a sign of good communication and can help improve communication. Whether it's hand-holding, back rubs, kissing, etc., physically connecting allows a couple to communicate without words. They get to know each other's nonverbal language on a deeper level.

Examples:

When you're watching a movie with your partner, sit with your legs touching.

Be physically close, like cuddling, without expecting sex.

When you're going for a walk, hold hands.

If your partner had a hard day and doesn't want to talk about it, offer to give them a back rub, foot rub, etc., instead.

When you're lying in bed relaxing, give your partner a head rub.

Always kiss and hug, "Hello" and "Goodbye."

They Listen To Each Other

We've talked a lot about active listening, especially in arguments, but listening outside of conflicts is a sign that a couple communicates well. A couple that listens to each other will remember what their partner likes and doesn't like, what they've asked them to do, and how they feel in certain situations. Neither feels like they always have to remind their partner about things, like chores or schedules. The same applies to body language; both people make an effort to notice nonverbal cues, so their partner doesn't feel that they always need to vocalize a feeling. They understand each other with a simple look or a touch, or at least pick up that their partner is trying to tell them something.

They Validate Each Other's Feelings

In a relationship built on empathy, the two people will validate the other's feelings as a top priority. This means not getting defensive and making excuses for behavior or words they don't like. Instead, there's a lot of active listening, putting themselves in their partner's shoes, and respecting what they feel. Even if they don't completely understand where their partner is coming from or feel what they're feeling, they never dismiss those emotions. The mere fact that their partner is feeling something is enough. In healthy relationships with good communication, this validating is a two-way street.

Examples:

While your partner is talking, maintain eye contact and give encouraging sounds or words, like "Hmm mm," "I see," and "I get that."

Direct your body towards them, instead of away, and keep it open, so they feel like you are there in the moment with them. If your partner likes physical touch, hold their hand, or rub their shoulder while they're talking about something that makes them emotional.

Ask follow-up questions so your partner knows you're still interested and committed to understanding what they're saying.

If you notice your partner acting differently, take the time to ask them if something is wrong and if they want to talk about it. This shows you are observant and not dismissive of what you see.

If they seem insecure or embarrassed about their feelings, validate them by saying something like, "Of course you feel that way" or "I would feel the same way, too."

They Aren't Afraid, To Be Honest, And Vulnerable

Honesty and vulnerability are essential in a healthy relationship. With couples who have good communication, opening up to each other isn't scary. A relationship is a safe place, not judgment, so both people feel comfortable talking about anything and being themselves. The significance of being honest and vulnerable with one's identity can't be overstated. This gets to the root of good communication and the positive power it can have over a relationship. When communication includes empathy, validation, and no judgment, both people feel secure in them and the actual relationship. This manifests as honesty and vulnerability.

They Are Flexible and Willing to Compromise

Seeing conflicts as puzzles to be solved together is enormous for a relationship. When communication is good, both people are more flexible and willing to compromise. They aren't stuck on a specific resolution they believe is the best one; they're open to their partner's input and finding a solution that makes both people happy. Arguments are much less likely to get heated and emotional when this is a priority.

They Can Take Accountability for Themselves

Couples who communicate well are not afraid to say two simple words: "I'm sorry." This phrase is short but incredibly powerful. It's a manifestation of an ability to take responsibility for one's actions and mistakes. It takes humility, which is a vital trait in any relationship. People can recognize when they're wrong and apologize let go of the need always to win. They can humble themselves before their partner and themselves. This type of "I'm sorry" isn't just skin-deep, either; it's a genuine apology that means the person is committing to being better in the future. A relationship between people willing to apologize and mean it will last way longer and be much more robust than relationships where that isn't a practice.

Examples:

When your partner points out something that annoys them, say something like, "Oh, I didn't know you felt that way; I'm sorry."

If you say something during an argument that you regret, come back to your partner and apologize, saying something like, "I feel terrible about what I said earlier, and I want to say I'm sorry. Following time, we're arguing; I'm going to try hard not to let that happen again."

If you can, be specific about the mistake(s) you made, saying something like, "I wasn't respectful of your feelings, and I'm sorry;" "I know you don't like it when I raise my voice, so I'm sorry for doing that;" and "I'm sorry I forgot to take out the trash this morning, I'll be sure to remember tomorrow."

CHAPTER 10 - How to Build Trust in Your Relationships?

Building trust in a relationship takes time, as well as a significant amount of effort. It is a work in progress, with its ups and downs. There will be days when you notice the difference and feel like the luckiest person alive. Your efforts are paying off. What you do matters. This is great.

On the opposite, there will be days when nothing seems to work. You hit a wall, and the shock is great. No matter what you do, things remain precisely the same. No progress whatsoever, nothing to hold on to. Yet, this is life. You need to be persistent and focus on the end goal, building a concrete fortress of trust for your relationship.

First of all, you must get ready to face the challenges daily. You are in for the long run, so you need to be consistent. It takes devotion to succeed in such an endeavor. Otherwise, everything you do on one day will be undermined by what you lack on the following day. Sending mixed messages can be catastrophic to your relationship, as it doesn't allow your partner to get a clear picture of what you want. This is why you ought to have a strategy planned to follow to get the best outcome. Think of the things to say and do, as much as the different reactions to emotional outbreaks. It is a long term commitment, so this is what you are up against. Routine can devour you unless you step up your game and claim what you deserve.

Acceptance is another concept you need to focus on. You need to accept people for who they are rather than who you are afraid they will be. You must understand the quality of the person standing right by your side. Who are you opening up to? Is that person indeed the one for you? Or are they playing you for a fool? If you notice any red flags, do not ignore or underestimate them. They will only get bigger over time, causing problems that are hard to tackle. Instead, be realistic and discover your partner's true self. I am sure you will love that, especially since your opinion will not be miles apart from a reality check. Once you accept a specific trait, you build your life around it, or you choose to flee.

Building trust in your relationships is a matter of patience. First, start small. Your partner needs to earn your trust, so put them to the test. It doesn't have to be something significant. Even the tiniest test will do. If he makes it to the following round, go bigger. Before you know it, you will have made it to the finish line. Life is not a constant struggle to prove a point. However, every day comes with different challenges. It is up to you how to react to those challenges, shaping your personality, and in a way shaping your relationship. There is nothing wrong with wanting to pass the test and expect our partner to do the same. You can share a secret and ask them not to tell anyone. Alternatively, you can request a favor, which shows how much they care. For example, driving you to the airport or going with you to the dentist's is a cool thing to do. If they end up being late or forgetting all about their commitment, this should put you on edge.

Learn from the past, as you have earned the right to do so. Each scar, each trauma, represents a badge you should wear with honor. Appreciate this valuable knowledge you have acquired over the years. Acknowledge these experiences, and implement the knowledge in your current state. You should feel proud of what you have accomplished, as well as what you have been through. All these experiences have made you who you are today. If you have suffered from a betrayal, a breach of trust in any way, a toxic relationship, sigh with relief that it is now over. Don't get drawn to the same mistakes now that you know better.

It is equally helpful to learn how to communicate with others openly. In this way, you will know how to tackle things as they come up. No matter if it is an emergency or a conflicting matter you need to talk about, do not postpone it. Be open and comforting, eager to make things right. Listen to the other side of the story, and let your partner know exactly how you feel. This is the only way you can move forward, leaving this all behind you. You cannot build trust in a relationship until the air has been clear from any hint of suspicion, misunderstanding, or misinterpretation.

Four basic principles act as pillars when building trust in a relationship. If you want to make the most of your relationship, evaluate these principles, and see if you are on the same page when honoring them and implementing them in your daily life:

- Honesty and integrity compose the first pillar. Without them, you cannot aim very high. You must be truthful and not hold back on what you want to say, even if they are not that good to hear. If your goal is to please others, then, by all means, do that. Still, this doesn't mean that you are building solid, reliable relationships with them. It is precisely the opposite. When your primary purpose for saying something is to distort reality in a way, then your relationship is bound to fail. Integrity is associated with expressing your opinion, no matter what. Instead of compromising your values and what you stand for, you need to be sincere and straightforward. No cutting corners, no beating around the bush. Be honest, and this is the best strategy for life.

- The second pillar is all about non-defensiveness. This might baffle you at first. Nonetheless, it is one of the most important things to aim at. You need to be realistic in your expectations from the relationship, both for you and your partner. In other words, you should not try to justify a wrong decision, nor should you criticize your partner with no ground. This is going to harm the relationship eventually. When you have second thoughts about talking to your significant other, the whole game has already been lost. Censorship is not the right way to go. Rather than filtering your words, make sure that you establish the basis of an honest, censorship-free relationship.

- Understanding should be self-explanatory, to be honest. You must practice understanding towards your partner, as well as expect the same treatment on their behalf. Actions have consequences, but there are also motives dictating us how to act in the first place. Consequently, you necessitate keeping an open mind. Learn how to be a good listener. Read in between the lines, discovering what drove your partner to act the way they did. You will be surprised to see that most things are justifiable. After all, there are always two sides in every story (at least). Do not rush to conclusions, but instead try to figure out how to empathize with your partner and resolve issues.

- Finally, use mutual understanding, respect, and love as a foundation to build a healthy relationship. It is direct communication that will make or break your relationship. How many times have you wondered if you should let your partner know about something straight away or if you should use a more strategic approach? Maybe ease into it, using tricks as your powerful weapon to achieve your goals? Although this can be more effective, it doesn't help your relationship. It teaches you how to be manipulative, even if you mean well. Invest in direct communication, telling what it is that is bothering you from the start. This pays off significantly in the end. Trust me!

CHAPTER 11 - Top Relationship-Strengthening Activities for Couples

When it comes to relationship issues, sometimes a couple cannot note a problem that may jeopardize their relationship's dynamics and functionality until the problem becomes evolved to the point where it appears to be drawing only more problems. That is why it is likewise essential to prevent these issues, which is most efficiently done with relationship-strengthening activities for couples. There is always more room for improvement, while your relationship should flourish as long as you are ready to make an effort and commit.

"Pillow Talks"

We can't emphasize enough how clear vital communication in relationships is. That is why our first relationship-strengthening activity on the list is dedicated to encouraging communication between couples. One of the best ways of practicing communication is to start with informal and "carefree" talk sessions. Suppose you are used to spending the evening alone but together. In that case, you may continue to read that journal you started with several days ago, and your partner is hooked to the TV or smartphone – you may decide to disconnect from lonesome activities and shut off the world while you focus on each other. You may lay down in bed or settle down on the sofa. It doesn't matter which location you choose –what matters is that you are not alone together. Start talking about your day, about your plans, start a conversation on anything that crosses your mind. Pillow talk topics may also revolve around affectionate talk, which is an excellent way of showing your partner's appreciation through verbal and non-verbal communication. Cuddling is also allowed as you talk, share opinions, and focus on what others have to say. This exercise helps you establish or re-establish a connection with your partner while practicing openness, communication, appreciation, and intimacy. Once you make these "pillow talks" your and your partner's routine, you might be surprised by how many new things you and your partner have found out about each other.

Mutual Interests and Hobbies

Although you and your partner may differ in preferences and characteristics, you indeed have some things in common. In case you start tracing similarities between your partner and yourself, you may be surprised with how many things you have in common. Everything you and your partner have in common can be used as an advantage in the process of improving your relationship. One of the best ways of intensifying your relationship is finding activities and hobbies that suit your mutual interests and focus on connecting through these activities. Instead of focusing on the ways you are different from one another, you should emphasize similarities that can serve the purpose of helping you reconnect with your partner while taking advantage of spending more time together through shared activities and hobbies.

"Who Are You?"

At the beginning of every relationship, your partner appears to be a perfect match, and everything you feel and see speaks in favor of the idea that you have found an ideal partner. As time passes, you are getting to know each other better, so both you and your partner are starting to notice flaws and characteristics that might get in the way of the "ideal." The fact is, there is no ideal. There is no perfection except a perfect imperfection – that means that you and your partner should be able to accept each other with flaws and traits; likewise, in case you truly love each other. Acceptance, recognition, and appreciation are critical qualities of a happy and healthy relationship. Don't be afraid to dig deeper, and don't be afraid to open yourself to your partner. One of the relationship-strengthening activities that may help you improve your relationship at the very start is getting to know each other better through a series of exercises for couples. For starters, you can exchange your favorite journals, play favorite music to each other, and agree to watch each other's favorite movies together. You may also get involved in quiz talk, asking your partner "trivia" questions that you believe would reveal a bit more about your partner's characteristics. For example, if you are watching a horror movie, you may ask your partner what his biggest fear is. Every shared activity with your partner is another way of getting closer to knowing each other better. By sharing your favorite journals, music, movies, and other personal things that your partner may be interested in, you share a piece of your characteristics and preferences, that way deepening intimacy and connection. Moreover, you are getting a hold of appreciation for the differences and similarities that describe you as a couple.

No Dwelling Allowed

Couples fight, argue, encounter disagreements, and tend to enter conflicts out of numerous different reasons –this is a perfectly normal thing in any relationship, including romantic relationships (perhaps, incredibly romantic relationships). Conflicts and disagreements arise as a way of testing a relationship's strength, while failing often means not putting enough effort into resolving problems you might have with your partner. Conflicts may "pack up" to create more serious issues and may result in losing the intimacy and connection you have with your partner, which furthermore may shake the very foundation of your relationship. Before you allow this to happen, you and your partner can work on preventive measures through couples' activities for strengthening. Whenever you and your partner enter a conflict or encounter a disagreement, make sure you can resolve this conflict and find an agreement before the end of the day and before you hit the bed. In case conflicts are left unresolved, you are tempted to dwell on the argument you are having with your partner, coming up with worst-case scenarios in your head and widening the gap between you and your partner. Instead of resolving the problem, some couples allow anger and dwelling to kick in, making the problem even worse and unattended, creating communication issues. To avoid making your conflicts worse, try to resolve your arguments within the same day you entered a conflict with your partner. Clear communication – talking and listening on turns while using logic and truth– is the best way of successfully resolving disagreements. If you cannot resolve a conflict with the same day the conflict started, you may agree to give the argument a rest for a couple of days until you can figure out whether the fight you are having is worth fighting in the first place.

Stressors: Identification and Elimination

We already talked about the effects that external factors and outside stressors can leave on a couple, along the way affecting the harmony and dynamics of your relationship. Stressors may test your relationship to the furthest points where it may even jeopardize it —however, there is something you and your partner can do to prevent that and make your relationship stronger. This activity will help you connect with your partner while learning how to appreciate each other's sensitivity and vulnerability to stressors. Moreover, this exercise should help you practice mutual support with your partner. Ensure that you can identify stressors and work on eliminating and diminishing external factors that are negatively affecting you, your partner, and your relationship. Stress factors should be identified and eliminated primarily because factors such as depression, illness, problems with finances, or problems at work can seriously damage your relationship. This is the case because we are sometimes stressed with numerous factors to the point where we are ready to vent our anger, insecurities, fear, and other negative emotions, regardless of whether it affects our partner's relationship. In case you are always stressed out, the chances are that you will release some of this tension at the cost of your partner's peace, which will push you into a conflict. Try to eliminate and identify stressors together with your partner to avoid negative case scenarios. It is perfectly acceptable to argue when there is a problem between you that needs to be resolved —however, venting due to the effects of stressors may only create a series of brutal conflicts until the real source of the problem is found and eliminated. For instance, if you are depressed, you need to talk to your partner about raising awareness that something is not quite right.

Moreover, you may find an ally in your partner to eliminate and identify the source of your depression. You may also choose to talk to a therapist about finding a solution. In case you have problems at work, instead of relieving your stress in a way that would affect your partner and your relationship, you may talk to your partner and ask for advice while letting your partner know that you have a problem causing you stress. When identified, any problem can be resolved while getting recognition, acceptance, and understanding from your partner will strengthen your relationship.

No Excuse for A "Busy" Life

So, you and your partner are committed to numerous obligations and might require superb multitasking skills to take care of everything you need to do in a day. As a consequence, you have little room for spending some alone time with your partner. This type of case scenario can lose a connection you have with your partner while emphasizing the lack of attention, appreciation, and intimacy. If you are too busy and always too tired to spend some alone time with your partner, you may unintentionally convince your partner that you don't care enough to commit. Regardless of how busy and hectic your everyday schedule may be, you NEED to find some time for your partner if you are motivated to keep your relationship alive and functioning. You can agree to spend more time together while setting up the mandatory day off from all other commitments to dedicate yourself to each other. Make sure to schedule at least one mandatory date a week –the more, the better.

Cuddling

Cuddling, kissing, kissing, holding hands – physical intimacy needs to be practiced through touch and physical connection. Forget about stress, obligations, and everything else that may act as a stressor or distraction, and enjoy your partner's company. Relationships grow stronger with enhanced intimacy as romantic relationships need physical connection —and that is a pure fact. The lack of physical intimacy may make your partner believe that she/he is neglected, doesn't matter to you. At the same time, it may also convince your partner that you are losing interest in your relationship. This is a relatively simple and rewarding activity for couples, and it asks only for free time and free will. Lie or sit beside your partner, hug each other, kiss, hold hands, cuddle —be physically intimate and enjoy these moments of bliss as you are working on strengthening your relationship.

CONCLUSION

Congratulations on making it to the end of this book.

Constant stress and anxiety can indicate that some parts of your life are off track and need to be changed. While your indications of nervousness can be difficult to control, putting aside some effort to investigate and trying to adjust to your discomfort, it could be a real open door to personal development. Whenever tension and insecurity strikes, think about what message they have for you and the potential changes you may need to make in your life. As opposed to continually being seen as a hindrance, they can help you feel progressively inspired and organized when viewed with difficulty.

With this book I hope I have encouraged you to strive to improve your life to make it happy and peaceful.

Good luck!

CPSIA information can be obtained
at www.ICGtesting.com
Printed in the USA
BVHW091524020621
608633BV00002B/72